Chalk Dust Memories
of the Good, the Bad, the Dying, and the Dead

Duane L. Schuman

`Copyright © 2015 Duane L. Schuman

All rights reserved

ISBN-13: 978-1517594039

Dedication

For all the students I was privileged to teach: the sick and the terminally ill; the gifted and the mentally challenged; those who were hard to reach and those who desired to learn; to those who thought they were unloved and those who knew they were loved; to the abused and the abusers; to those whose barriers I was able to penetrate and those who always trusted me and those I coaxed to write as well as those who wrote proficiently for me. You were a great part of my life and I remember you still. You are my inner voice for you were with me more that half my life.

Table of Contents

Dedication	page 4
PART ONE ' THE STUDENTS	page 5
PART TWO: FAMILY MEMORIES	page 51
PART THREE	
Pet Peeves	page 75
Stand Outs: Old Teachers	page 81
Death Intrudes	page 83
Thinking Back	page 85
Me and Religion	page 88
Hinterland Recall	page 91

Duane L. Schuman

Chalk Dust Memories of the Good, the Bad, and the Dying and the Dead

Part One: The Students

Over the years I have written many poems and some novels as well as short stories drawing upon what I personally heard or encountered dealing with teens and the world into which they tried to muddle through. Whether it was a western, fiction, or science fiction there were some kernels of truth sprinkled in from my days as an educator.

"I can't!"; "I don't know how!"; "It's hard!" are some of the rebuttals teens had given me over the decades for most of the school subjects they found frustrating-and writing was certainly not one of their exceptions.

This is a compilation of some of those students' writings, my thoughts about them, and the various problems they brought to the learning environment with them. They had very conceivable disability ranging from the low functioning mentally retarded to the health impaired with regular or exceptional abilities. Without exception each expressed their thoughts on paper. Some did it articulately and very well while others just barely managed, but they shared their innermost, private thoughts with me, their teacher.

With nearly 38 years of students to choose from and a variety of problems I decided to select those whose faces I can still see and voices I can hear if I try to listen as I contemplate them, whether I have any examples of their work or not.

These then are the stories of the sweet or mean, the sick or dying, those who shared their life with me and those not trying.

After spending nearly four decades trying to educate children I came to the realization that there are many things that the public never sees or is made aware of. There are many realities that teachers must deal with on a daily basis that seldom are considered newsworthy enough to make the newspapers. Among these are the living conditions in which the students arrived at school having escaped and wishing only that they didn't have to return to the same squalid, filthy, dangerous "home" in the evening after school was over. Inner-city children can't leave their real problems at home.

They bring them with them into the school with themselves daily. Unless you have visited them in their home setting, you would not believe the horrible home environments they flee daily-when they are physically able. It was not uncommon to have to teach these students in infested homes where the roaches were so plentiful you felt filthy just having to sit at the kitchen table, much less watch student papers move across the table because of the roaches underneath. Then on the other side of the coin is the home filled with feces, pet feces strewn all over which no one swept away, especially horrendous in those homes without furniture where you would have to sit on the floor in the clearest spot you could find. So the main problems I found students dealing with at home were vermin, fecal matter, and little or no furniture. Very few school employees really know what goes on in the minds of children who suffer abuse daily in all its many forms. Over the years I have seen or dealt with most abusive problems that any student might have encountered. Some students who were intellectually able to did put aside their emotional hurts long enough to write about what was bugging them or preventing them from getting a good night's sleep so they can stay awake during school classes.

There is some information about the single parent family trying to make ends meet while providing for their children and this information generally focuses on the single mother. There are some single fathers trying to do the same thing; however society seldom mentions them, but I have had several trying their best to provide for special need children. And nothing is mentioned about the fathers of special needs children who stay in the family's life and try to maintain the family unit providing stability even though the horrendous bills would drive men of lesser moral stature to leave. I watched one family stay together, become poorer and poorer monetarily as the medical bills piled up. The dad quit a high paying job that took him out of the state in order to be home with his child, and though the cancer raged he did not. He was the father figure that child needed, especially at that time. They did not lose their faith but drew closer to each other relishing the times their child could smile. They let their own health slide being so involved with their child's. The mom died suddenly of a bleeding ulcer but father and son carried on. Though the father would pass soon, the son never lost his faith. Choosing to have some quality of life rather than quantity (of a few extra months) this young man did the things he and his parents couldn't while they fought the cancers in his body. Before he died, he told me he was happy and content: he had enough money to take care of his expenses with some left over." What more could anyone ask for?" he said to me knowing death would come for him soon.

When I was a child going to school, a fight was a rare occurrence and the worst violence that would impact a child at school. By the time I started teaching in the 70s, fights were fairly commonplace and we teachers often were needed to break up these fights. And now girls were involved too. One of the first girls I taught in Homebound was a girl who had been stabbed by another girl and run down. When they saw her getting up they ran her over again. She only sustained a broken leg and was ready to return to school to have her turn. Some of the nastiest fights I ever saw were between two girls with their rakes or combs. Students now carried knives, numchuks and other assorted weapons to school and were not afraid to show or use them. Guns were not too common, but adolescent stupidity did reign supreme. On my campus during lunch some students got into their car, but instead of going off campus to eat, they decided to play Russian roulette. The result was that one blew his brains all over the car! I never saw nor heard anything about that incident in the news. I only was aware of it because it happened on my campus!

When I changed from a classroom teacher to a teacher of Homebound students, I soon discovered how easy it could be for students to get guns if they wanted them. Students weren't afraid to speak about how easy it would be for them to go to a particular corner and come away with what was then known as a "mid-night special." Then it was a term used for a cheap gun purchased after dark illegally. One of my students had an AK47 with the ATF treasury certificate issued to his mother. He intended to open a place similar to Shooter's Palace with money held in trust because of a botched surgery.

      As the decades passed and we entered a different century, the violence continued to escalate. Kids and teachers no longer feel safe when they are at school since the madness abounds everywhere now and death can stalk them in the classroom just as easily as it used to on the city streets and so they retaliate in doing drive-bys, hoping to kill the enemy first. During this time period one of our district's special education's teachers was brutally stabbed by one of her students. One of my student's sisters was raped in her bed and killed so they fled the city the next day. Another student received a drive-by which narrowly missed killing his mother. They moved that next day but he said he knew who did it and the police wouldn't have to find them. He wouldn't listen to anything I would say. All he could see were the 17 shell casings in the street and the holes in their house.

I realize the world these kids find themselves in is not a happy world to grow up in any more. Whether it occurs in a mall, on a campus, in a church or at home, senseless killing seems to be growing and the ones sworn to protect sometimes are the ones we need protecting from. It's a world in turmoil and children are still expected to learn and thrive. That is the insanity of our culture.

Duane L. Schuman

The group of students that impacted me the most were the students who contracted some form of **cancer**. The first student I lost as her teacher was not yet 16. Her parents had the foresight to plan ahead and had an early "Sweet Sixteen" party before she died ten days later. Though **S**** was the first, she wasn't the last student I lost to some form of cancer. The others I am sure passed on because of their cancers or complications were **A**, A**, A**, D**, Ch**, E**, G**, S**, S**, and S****. These are the stories they and other cancer victims shared. I use the * and the Initial of their first name to protect the anonymity of these students. All errors are as they wrote them.

A** was stricken during the summer and couldn't understand why he had to develop **cancer.** He was lucky because a bone-marrow donor match was found: his little sister. Though he said he'd rather his brother had been the match, he was proud of his sister because he knew the pain she would go through merely because she loved him. He wrote about his feelings quite well.

"Shocking News

Working full time and spending my money on my car were my goals for this summer. But all that changed a week later. I found out I have **leukemia.** The day I found out I had leukemia my whole life changed. I was admitted into the hospital. The doctor said I could have died. I asked, "Why me?" But nobody could answer that for me. My doctor has a road map for me. It's a plan on what kind of treatment I'll get and the medication I'll be taking. Some days I was ok with the pain. Other days everything would make me angry. I didn't want to do anything. All I could think about is going home and wanting to be my normal self. On these days my parents were always there to remind me if I wanted to go home, I had to take my medicine and do everything the doctors and nurses asked me to do. It sounds easy but it's so hard. While I was getting **chemotherapy** during my stay, the doctors sent my mother and sister for tests to see if either of them would be able to be my bone marrow donor. My little sister is my match. If I had it my way it would have been my brother. Don't get me wrong, it's not because she's a girl. She is so fragile and I don't want her in pain. Overall I am lucky to have a little sister who is helping me treat cancer."

H** had **testicular cance**r, which was ever so devastating for any male, yet he found solace and strength to endure. He was lucky enough and the cancer was overcome.

"Dealing with Cancer

The way I deal with **cancer** is thru my family which are always there for me. Most especially my mom who has been there with me in every step of the way. during the bad times that I fell really sick. Another person who has helped me is my church's pastor, who always reassures me that I'm going to be all right."

S** suffered from chronic ,pain which they finally discovered was not just in her head but a **neurosarcoma**, which is a malignant peripheral nerve sheath tumor or a cancer of the tissue that surrounds the nerves.

"Comparison/Contrast of *Hop Frog* and *Cask of Amontillado*

There are many comparisons and contrasts contained in *Hop Frog* and *The Cask of Amontillado*. Edgar Allen Poe writes both stories with a central theme of revenge. Both stories deal with revenge, there is also the aspect of romance in Hop Frog.

In *The Cask of Amontillado* the revenge wasstrictly for the sake of Montgressor who had taken Fortunado's insults until he could be avenged. Whereas, in *Hop Frog* the revenge was not planned fully until the King cheered on by his council, had abused Hop Frog's friend and most likely love interest, Trippetta.

In both stories the antagonist set their own demise. Both Fortunado and the King were set up for revenge by the very thing they cared most about, liquor and joke, respectively. Fortunado's demise was set in private and the King's demise was public

Montressor enjoyed his revenge alone, while Hop Frog enjoyed his revenge with his love, Trippetta-so it was thought."

S** had **bone cancer**. Like most teens she would bend the truth when her mother asked questions about what she was to be doing for homework but she would eventually get it done.

"The Grossest Thing

The grossest thing on the human body. It's their feet because they may toe jam and make stuff with it. Their toes may not be clean, and Toe People may said, "Get me your toe and you may have to run away from them and they will get you and they may eat your toe up and said that are good toes but not good they will put your toes ion the trash and said those are not good toes. Those are bad toes and then you have to clean your toes. Just ask little Johnny and is the grossest thing on the human body."

S** B** died from **Ewing Sarcoma**, a type of cancer generally found in the bone or soft tissue of girls. He was another unusually bright young man who never lost his faith and was a delight to all who met and taught him.

"Predator

What a wonderful smell! The smell of the morning means that the zebras are awake, which in turn means breakfast. I suppose they will be grazing in the same field as yesterday because the grass is plentiful and lush. I won't make the same mistake I did yesterday. Today, I get there early enough so they won't see me sneak up. After a quick bath in the river, I will head out for breakfast.

On the way to the field, I saw a delicious looking rabbit. It looked very tasty, but I left it alone because I had to focus on the bigger prize: a field of zebras. When I finally got to the field, I found it empty as planned. Now it was time to play the waiting game. I waited and waited for hours, but the zebras didn't come...

Finally, after many hours of waiting, the zebras came! I made sure that I was completely hidden from view and got ready to attack. Any second the zebras would walk into their own death. I carefully scanned the area for the fattest zebra and found him about ten yards away. I immediately jumped up and ran as fast as

I could toward the zebra. All of the zebras were shocked to see me and stood frozen in terror. I quickly jumped on him and bit him dead. I not only got the fattest zebra that day, but also a very tasty rabbit."

E** P** probably had the most profound effect upon my life and the writing of my students I have served over the decades. Although he and his parents died long ago, I can still hear and see them. Though he wrote a lot, I chose to incorporate these as examples of his caring, searching spirit. He suffered from **rhabdomyosarcoma** first and a secondary and harder to overcome cancer **A.L.L. Acute Lymphatic Lymphoma,** yet remained positive throughout his ordeal.

Myself

My name is E** __son
Working at NASA is one of my goals
To be working there would be fun
To design a spaceship and its hulls.
I won an award for Murphy's Law
Because of my bad luck streak.
It really wasn't one of my calls,

So it looks like I'm up the creek.
I work with Legos and have a base
With many ships and their crews.
And this base is set up in space
To some that might not even be news.
I sometimes have trouble making a rhyme.
Though that you may not see;
But now I seem to be out of time-
Thus ends this poem about me."

"My View on Life

      Some people may think of my situation as unfortunate. I do not. In fact, I find my life quite lucky. I'm an American citizen living in the land of opportunity. I always have a roof over my head, many people across the world don't I always have food, many people die of starvation every day. I have warm and comfortable clothes. I have a government that cares enough about me to give me a disability because of my condition. I'm getting an education, and my house has many items that are quite a luxury when you consider it.
      So many things I have that many in the world do not. One of my biggest advantages in my mom and dads .Without them I would have died years ago. My mom has a lot of medical knowledge she has put to use to

save me multiple times My dad's great strength I can, and do, draw from. Just that they're together is another thing I have.

So what if I have **cancer**? When you think about it, I'm no closer to death than anybody else. Mine is just more obvious. At any time anyone can be called home by God be it a car accident, heart attack, or something else. And when it's your time, it's your time. God could send a semi truck through the house to recall me if he wants to.

Don't get me wrong, overall I'd definitely prefer not to have it. I do miss being able to go out in public without worrying about who is near me and whether they have been near anyone sick. I also miss having the energy a normal person has. Other things I miss too. But with that being taken away I have gained things. My perspective on life that I'm writing about right now is one example. There are people out there seemingly with everything that are miserable. My family (by that I mean my parents) and I are happy. Every day we joke and laugh, and enjoy life. My mom once complained about turning 44. I told her about how my current goal was to live to be 32. I told her that for me, it would be great to make it to 44 and beyond. She says her view on aging has been forever changed from that.

Another gain is life on computers. Before cancer, the only computers I have ever been on was one at school and an old (the year I was born) From Make-a-Wish I got an up to date one, and fell in love with the world of computers. With them I can write stories, research anything I wish (I found some fascinating information on nanotechnology the other day), play games, meet interesting people, and countless other things.

So, as you can see, I am quite lucky. Sure, my life has a couple of bumps in it, but **God has given them to me for His own reasons. I may not know them, but I can handle it. and handle it I will."**

"Mr. Schuman
I remember early days of him coming by,
I was too sick to do anything but lay there
Yet he gave me some work just asked that I try,
And I did what I could, all I could bear,
When the doctors said I was going,
He brought an elder and over me prayed.
That night there was quite a showing
As my death was indefinitely delayed.

Over the years he's been constantly there,
More than a teacher, he's been a close friend
Our writing works with each other we share
And now my schooling is nearing an end.
`Ah, Mr. Schuman, what to do now?
You've been coming by for six years
But keep in contact we will somehow
No matter the turns our paths may veer."

The next group are the **school phobics.** They differ from your average truant in that the very thought of going to school makes them sick. I served only two of these (and three others who were just truant): **A** and S**.** Of those who were truants, one was always out walking the streets after curfew. With a dream of owning as place like Shooters' Palace, he got his mother to legally purchase a large assortment of weapons in her name with all the appropriate ATF paperwork. He was proud of the collection and showed it to me one afternoon.

A** was served by everyone in my department. She practiced selective mutism meaning she talked when she wanted to. She reminded me a great deal of another student, **B**** who I had in my Resource class because she was supposedly legally blind, however, she would sit on a stool with a pad of paper in her lap, writing quite legibly Though her eyesight had improved greatly, she liked the comfort of the small class setting and maneuvered adults into getting what she wanted until my observations. Sensing this in **A**** I got her father on my side and he made sure she was up and ready for school before he had to leave for work. Though obviously mentally challenged, she managed to play her parents and the system the way she wanted. However, we finally managed to get her to start writing though I found out she played games with her mother and got her way when her father's job changed and he could not be there to ensure her getting up.

"Belonging (original)
She belonging to me
At home for
Finally She's our cat We
Like her name

Is Rosie She saved me She plays
With each of us **A**** I
Love her she's a
Mine She makes me
Happy. To see her is
Fun See mine lonely
She lives with us She's
Not lonely"
[corrected version
She belongs to us at home for
Finally she's our cat. We like her.
Her name is Rosie. She saved me.
She plays with each of us. A**
loves her. She's mine.
She makes me happy.
To see her is Fun. See mine
lonely. She lives with us.
She's not lonely.]

DIABETES TYPE 1 was the first time I realized this disease attacked children and was prevalent among teens. Over the decades I only served four teens for whom it was the only factor impinging on their ability of going to school: **B**, LaQ**, LaT**, and A****. As in adults it can lead to lots of other health and social problems.

B** was giving herself 6 **injections of insulin** daily. Her outlook on life was usually positive but her behavior always got her in trouble. That's when she'd stop taking the insulin she'd end up in the hospital.

"The Way I See Myself
I see myself as a good person to get along with. I don't think I am all that great in looks, but I know I am pretty. And as time goes by I know I'll grow older and into a prettier and better woman each and every day.
I don't know everything about life, but what I do know makes me what I am each day of my life. And as long as I follow God and trust in him with all my heart and soul I know that I am the best person that I can be. That's the way I see myself."

A** was an adolescent **diabetic** who admitted she experimented with drugs and was sorry she did.

Duane L. Schuman

"The Story of My Life (edited)[self[

I became sick a lot as a child. I had major ear infections and had tubes put in my ears and later taken out because of more infection. I began drinking water and juices excessively. My parents took me to the doctor...it took a year for a diagnosis but the doctors found out that I had a risease called **Histiocytosis X**. This is a disease of the immune system where white blood cells are attacking each other and leaving lesions or damaging other parts of my body. This disease left lesions in my head and caused damage to my pituitary gland, which caused another rare disease called **diabetes insipidus**. **Diabetes insipidus** is a water diabetes which requires hormone replacement. Since my body doesn't produce the anti-diuretic hormone (ADH), I have to take the medicine. Due to the medicine, I have been on and off chemo most of my life.

The middle of my freshman year I got hooked up with some of the wrong people and started taking a drug called **ice** and I smoked a little weed. I later went through drug rehab and straightened out that part of my life. However, I took up smoking real cigarettes, another mistake. I smoked a couple of years off and on then I found out through a checkup that I had **pulmonary LCH.** It never seems to stop. This required **more chemo** which I am still going through today. If I could share with others, I would tell them that drugs and cigarettes are not cool"

Illnesses and other diseases I have classed together under the groupings of: **Chronic Immune Deficiency Syndrome, Renal problems, and Miscellaneous diseases and illnesses.**

CIDS: I only served two teens who had **CIDS.** Both were young ladies who were quite smart. Both were almost always upbeat, did their work to the best of their ability and looked forward to returning to school

E**

"All about Me

I am 18 years old and consider myself still a baby. At least that's the way

I'm treated, but I don't mind 'cause we All know babies get the best treatment.

At this point of my life I am very happy with myself. I know most teenagers would be unhappy if they had to suddenly get out of school their senior year, but I'm not. Don't get me wrong. I love being in school and as soon as I can return, I will.

I have just realized what means the most to me, and that would be my education. As long as I am getting one it shouldn't matter where it's at whether it's here at home or at school.

My family is my life. We are very close and I would say they are my inspiration. They have really shown me the way a family should be. I couldn't go on without them, They are my friends. They listen to me, help me, and most of all care for me. I am grateful.

As for myself, I am really a happy-go-lucky kind of girl. At least that is what I have been referred as. I am a great friend, and I believe the reason for that is because I will do anything for my friends to help them. I love being able to help people and that goes for strangers as well.

I am really just the average teenage

girl am really just the. I just have a little illness that doesn't keep me from anything too long."

Of the four or five students who had **kidney problems** two stand out for their positive outlook despite dialysis and transplants: **M** AND L****. Decades later, they still leave a positive imprint upon me.

L** is a musically gifted young man who loves to play piano. He is the only student I have had who does his **Dialysis** at home while he sleeps.

"Kidney Problems

Kidney problems galore, that's what I've got. It started when I was itty bitty. First it was my bladder, then that went on to affect my kidney. Yes, I only have one. I was born with it, so don't ask me. I get tired of people asking what happened, why, blah-blah. It's just B.S. But I know that most of them care about me and want to make sure that I'm doing alright. It gets a little annoying sometimes, but I just smile and keep on answering. **Dialysis** is a drag. Hopefully, sometime soon I will get to spend the night somewhere besides my own bed. But you never know. My stomach looks like a war zone. The scars are unbelievable. I have two tubes hanging out of me, which doesn't really impress the girls that much. Still it is kind of weird how most of them like me. There is this one that is obsessing. She almost started to cry tonight at church because I was with my girlfriend instead of her. I would go out with her, but she is a little too young, and I already have a girlfriend that I like a lot. Well, I am kind of getting off track so I will shut up now,"

"Worst Day
　　The worst day I ever experienced was the day I woke up and was having trouble walking. I couldn't figure out what was wrong with me so just left it alone. I got up and did my usual morning routine. Then I went into the living room and watched tv. I got tired of this very quickly so I went into my sister's room to play the piano. When I sat down, I put my hands on the keys, but I couldn't play. My fingers weren't moving.

That's when I knew it was serious. I waited for my mom to get home and talked to her about it. By this time, I couldn't walk at all. So she rushed me to the emergency room and found out my potassium was very low. I got to stay in the hospital for about a week to get it back up. Then I GOT TO GO HOME. That was the worst day of my life because I thought I might never play the piano again."

M** was an orthopedically handicapped student who had a fatalistic view of life: what will happen, will happen. Knowing that black kidney donor matches were rare, he expected to be on dialysis until he died, probably within the next ten years. However he expected nothing but to be treated fairly with dignity and respect.

"My Trip to the Doctor

Today I am going to the doctor for a checkup. I am going today at 3:00 o'clock. I start to wheel myself outside to the car. Then I got into the car and my mom started taking my wheel chair apart to put it inside the car. She began by taking off one of the wheels of the chair and then the other wheel and the handle bars. She put the wheel chair pieces in the car. And then we were on our way to the doctor. It took 30 minutes to get there. A d then we got out of the car went inside to sign in sat down for almost 45 minutes before we were called. He showed us to the back of the room. He looked at my foot and gave me some cream for my foot and we were on our way back home and that was my trip to the doctor."

"The Worst Day of My Life

I went to the doctor for a checkup. It was May 30, 2004. It was a sunny day. My mom got out of the car so she could put my wheel chair together. She put the wheels on followed by the brakes. Then she helped me to get in the chair to walk up to the doctor's office. We had to wait for almost an hour before we could see him. We went into this room. It took him 5 minutes to come into the room. Then he took some blood from me and said to come back the next day for the results. When we did I was told my kidneys were not working and I needed to have **dialysis** 3 times a week until I could get a new kidney. That was the worst day of my life."

The last group of various illnesses and diseases includes: **spina bifada, stroke, uterine problems, pregnancy, seizures disorders, allergies, hernias, sickle cell, meningitis, heart problems, burns, lupus, migraines, hemophilia, hepatitis, and mononucleosis.** There was also one case of **H-IV positive** that I would discover after the fact.

Though he suffered from **spina bifada, A**** was able to maneuver his wheel chair throughout his apartment with an amazing agility. Writing he said,
"You didn't know that I was born in Dallas. I moved to Pittsburgh in Kindergarten where my grand- parents bought a resort. We stayed there about 4 years til my mom picked me up from school one day and said we were moving to Michigan. We moved there about a month til our dad came and got us. So we went back to Pittsburgh to live with my alcoholic father for another year. My parents were going through a divorce. My dad was abusive so my mom worked awfully hard to get us out of that house. We were stuck there for

another year while my dad beat us. Finally, the court date came up and the judge asked us where we wanted to live. So we were allowed to go back with our mom. We had to stay with my grandma who threw us out shortly after. So we were forced to go to a women's shelter in Dallas where I learned what street violence was. We didn't go a day without hearing a gunshot. That's when I decided it was time to start lifting weights. I was tired of getting beat up all the time. So I kept to myself, getting stronger until the eighth grade where I got into my first fight and I wasn't defending myself. I was standing up for someone else. That changed my life. For the first time I had some respect. From then on I never got beat up again and we haven't moved much. I'm finally making a few friends so things are starting to look up."

D** was unusual in that he was extremely **allergic to mold** they found in his school . Since that particular mold did not affect anyone else, the school district decided that it was cost-effective to have him taught at home rather than tear up the whole school.

"A Reflective Poem

Procrastinate
Why not wait a while?
Take my time; do it much later
Why be in haste?
Procrastinate."

E**, Though suffering from **severe asthma**, coughed up blood and they found she had a **hernia**.

"My Worst Day

My worst day was when I got sick. I was over at my sister's house. My feet started to swell, and I started to **cough up blood**. A couple of days later when my mama came to get me, I could barely walk. I couldn't even get my shoes on. The cold got worse. I could hardly breathe. My mother soaked my feet in some Epsom salt. It went down. My mama did that for like 3 days. I started taking antibiotics for a week and some night quelled for my coughing. When I went to my granny's house, she got me an inhaler for my breathing so that I could breathe well. I still be coughing up blood and if I sit with my feet hanging down too long, they will swell. I'll be okay on the worst day because my family loves me and always around me. So my worst day was when I was sick."

"I am a Teardrop

I'm a teardrop on a sad day. I could even be joyful too. I come wen you're sad. I even come when they're glad. You can wipe me away with your hands and you could wipe me away with a piece of tissue. Everyone sees me sometime. I'm part of an emotion. I'm here on the first day of school. I'm here when a loved one dies or when your son or daughter have taken their first step. I could be dark or light. I come even when there's a fight. I'm here pretty often for different reasons. They don't have to be bad. They could be good. I can make a baby fall asleep. I'm here when the baby's born or you get sick. I'm a teardrop on a sad day. I'm everywhere: in the army, at the church, on the first day of birth. I could make your eyes red and puffy. I can drop a whole lot or just a little bit. I'm a teardrop."

N** was stricken with **meningitis, an inflammation of the brain and/or the spinal chord;** however his real problem was coming to terms with his **grief** over the death of his brother. Writing was a good catharsis for him.

"Losing Someone Special

Losing family members is something that people never forget even if you are far apart. But losing a family member that is close, like a brother or sister, is devastating. I didn't just lose my brother, but I lost my best friend as well. He was always there for me no matter what the problem was. For instance, hooking up radio systems. It would always be just us two, and when we were finished, it made us happy because we achieved something together. After it was all connected, we would go and wash the car and take it to a car show to show off what we created, hoping to win a trophy.

Also, when I would go to work with him, we would paint houses and have

fun while we were supposed to be working. Most of the time we wouldn't work but just play around with the spray gun or drive around in the work van listening to the radio.
These were just some of the things I did with my brother, but now he's not around to do that anymore. Now you see why I miss him so much, and the times we had together will never be forgotten."

S** B** was the only student I had undergoing **skin grafts** for burns previously suffered. About a third of each finger is gone leaving his hands barely able to hold a pencil, yet he can write with one. Although the shell he resides in is far from perfect his wit, sagacity, and determined inner strength shine through.

"Trust is the virtue I hold above all else, not first from others but from myself.
My inhibitions are low, my standards are high.
`Live for today and tomorrow who knows when I'll die
Love my family, I love my friends

I try to treat them fairly and hope they'll be there in the end.

When I die, I want people to say "Gosh what a great guy," because losers are born every day.

I believe that I know the meaning of life. I believe life is about being truly happy. True happiness can mean anything from changing tires to raising a family to try to end world hunger. Life isn't about what you've accomplished. Life is about being a good person in every aspect. Religion takes my part. If there is someone upstairs then he'll know what's going on."

As you would expect, over the years I have come in contact with several students suffering from a myriad of **broken bones, survived wrecks, and related surgeries; including arms skulls, femurs, knees, legs ,and even backs.**

J** broke his **femur** while he was skateboarding

> Pyramid
> Through thick and thin
> We should stick together no matter
> Whatever is bad or worse, it's a bond
> You can't break-blood
> Like father and like son
> Family."

J**y was first student I ever had with a **halo around his head** though I have had students with them around their ankles. Like others he wrote in order to grieve

> "Sad Event
> A sad event that happened in my life

occurred this past June when one of my close friends died in a car accident. Also my cousin passed away 3 years ago when he was mugged and killed outside a nightclub in St Louis. With both events including death, it was heartbreaking.

    I remember it was Saturday morning when I heard about Johnny's death. I was up watching some cartoon. Then the phone rang, and I picked it up. It was my aunt Lily (Johnny's mother) She asked to talk to my mother so I handed her the phone. During the time my mom and her sister were talking, I was pretty happy she called because I thought they were coming to town. Then I saw my mom in tears, and I just knew right away that something was wrong. They let each other go, that is, they mutually hung up the phones and she told me what had happened. At that time I was really sad, upset, and angry all at the same time. That Wednesday we left for Missouri. His funeral was on Saturday. This event was sad to me because a loved one had passed on. Johnny and I didn't hang out much because of the distance, but we were close. He was a good guy and friendly. I just can't imagine who could do such a thing.

June 17, 2002 was the day that changed my life forever. I was involved in a fatal car accident. I was wounded badly along with Valy. He was hurt most of all of us. At the hospital he passed on the next day. I was still in ICU. I was asking about Valy's condition, and everyone kept telling me he was fine. I understand why everyone lied to me. It was because I had a lot of surgery coming up and they didn't want me to worry or stress out about it. When my mom told me the truth, I started crying. Feeling really bad, blaming myself for his death. I can't write any more but these are the sad events that happened the past few years."

R** P** was slapped in the face with his friend's, death, his parents' divorce, and his father's suicide so **healing from a wreck** was just part of his convalescence since he was another who needs to grieve.

"June Jinx

June is the worst month for me. The past two years in the month of June, I have had so much horrifying things happen to me. Jun e 19, 1997 our scout troop was on our way back from Philmont. During Philmont I got a letter saying that my parents were getting a divorce. That ruined the rest of my trip. Then on my way back on June 19, the car ahead of us from our troop rolled 5 times, They were about 15 minutes in front of us. The turmoil that the wreck caused was unbelievable. One of my friends died. He was only 16. Two others were seriously hurt. They were brothers. Then this year in June three major things occurred. On June 2, 1998 my dad committed suicide. He didn't even leave a letter. Actually, he did leave one thing, a son without a father. About a week later I **wrecked t**he truck that my dad bought me earlier. Then on June 25, 1998 I was riding shotgun in one of my friend's cars. He lost control, rolled it, knocked down some trees, and wrapped it around another one. I was **in the hospital for a month.** That is the June Jinx."

Special education coded students in danger of failing often ended in homebound. I have worked with the **emotionally disturbed, learning disabled, visually handicapped, auditorially handicapped, traumatically brain injured, orthopedically handicapped, and other health impaired.** At one tine we also served students who were adjudicated. Some were serve d injail while waiting trial or sentencing and some in other places as Court Appointed **Clear and Present Danger**

C** , a mentally challenged student was so down on herself that at first she kept looking down into her lap and would hardly talk above a whisper. Though that changed, she refused to write saying she couldn't. However, after much cajoling she would answer my questions and write her answers on paper which made succeeding assignments easier.

"Songs are music that flows in the air. So0me have a melody. It moves fast. I like to hear them.

Animals are little creatures that crawl on the earth. You have all kings. You got your cats and dogs and birds, and hippos, and monkeys, and snakes there all different colors.

I like cats Cats are nice people that walk and roam in the street. Some are white and some are black. There very quiet."

Because the Homebound Department was under the auspices of Special; Education, we served everyone including court ordered, **clear and present danger** students along with regular special education coded students and the general population, **We were all things to all people**. The **Clear and Present Danger** category included students suspected of murder or attempted murder, felonious assault on a teacher as well as those involved in fights and other aggressive acts.

` **R****, though one of the most dangerous and violent bi-polar students I ever served, was basically just a frustrated, unwanted youth. Regardless of the seriousness of the charges against him, we met in an open room, not some confined space and without any special guidelines for me or any aides present for my protection either. It was just him and me in this large room.

"I threw a **4 x 4 through a window at school and a teacher got cut by the glass** and I ran away the cops picked me up and took me to **Kimbo Road lock up** center for twenty for hours and now the school wants to expel me so until I find out what they're going to do I'm stuck here at home bound school

I hate school. I'm a nice guy and like to make jokes sand that I like animals I hate school it sucks

I'm going to drop out as soon as I turn 17 nobody is going to get in my way. I hate school and that's that. I'm going to be a high school drop out.

Places I've Been
Terrell State Hospital: locked there for 6 to 9 months it was hell I was always in the QR (quite room) or in bed restraints so my stay there was long and boring.

San Antonio State Hospital: I was only there for about a week but that made me straighten my s*** up the Staff were cruel they beat the kids gave them smokes the female staff F*** the boys there its just not a good place to go

CBYC I was there over a year it was cool; at first we went to the beach on the weekends went to Houston on vacation it was cool until I got to know the place then I screwed up and started using drugs and running away. Then they kicked me out."

G,another clear and present danger student,** was basically good until he got involved with **gangs** in middle school. He still had **2 bullets** in him from the last shooting when I saw him after a drive-by unloaded some 17 bullets at his house, narrowly missing his mother in the front bed room; the family moved.

"My Life Story

Duane L. Schuman

When I was little I never grew up with my dad. Till this day I never seen him by flesh or by pictures. When I was a little kid I use to run down the street naked chasing ice cream man my family always use t laugh at me cause of that But also my mom always use to kill chicken in the back yard one time she cut off a chicken head and the chicken took off running with no head. I still remember that I also remember I was walking on a board and fell off and was hanging cause I had gotten cough with a nail. It made me a big cut on my armpit. I still got that scare But expecially when I was little I was nice I used to clean up the houses and sometimes cook for myself. I always use to cry when it got cloudy couse I was scare of tornadoes. But my mom was always there for me Everybody loved me But everything change when I went to middle school. I got introduce to gang that is when everybody of my family not start to like me no more. But what I remember most is when I went to Mexico to go see my grama she told my mom couple before she died that I was going to kill my mom. That hurt a lot to this day I don't k now what she meant by that..."

Well after that drive-by where one of the bullets hit a few inches above where his mom lay sleeping, he knew. This one made a real impression and the family moved.

B y the time I was forced to retire due to health issues Homebound teachers had been relegated from coming up with the lesson plans and doing the teaching to basically ferrying the home school teacher's lessons and desires for the student. We were there to help explain the lesson, not to teach.

A**t suffered from **hemophilia**. His parents maintained a small refrigerator in the apartment above the garage that they had remodeled for him. He went through $20,000 of medicine a month in the 80s. His loving family did everything possible to make things easier for him. At the end of the Spring semester the father confessed to me the reason his son looked so pale was that he had become **H-IV POSITIVE** as a result of transfusions, a secret they had kept from everyone outside the immediate family because of the stigma attached to it then. It didn't help them knowing he got it from a dirty needle. I'm just glad I didn't over react though they had put me and my own family at risk by not knowing.

Duane L. Schuman

Chalk Dust Memories:
Part Two: Family Memories

My first taste of cancer was early in my teaching career. Though I taught Special Education, I had a regular education homeroom. One of my homeroom students, a beautiful girl named **L**** developed cancer in her lymph nodes and when they reoccurred she would miss a lot of school as they fought the cancer spreading to the lymph nodes throughout her body. My last taste of it so far was my own father who had cancer of the larynx and stomach probably caused by his smoking.

Smoking has claimed a number of victims in my family. Both my mother and father were heavy smokers. I can't remember ever seeing a picture of my mother without her having a cigarette in her hand. My Uncle Lou and Grandpa "Buck" were also heavy smokers. Mom's smoking led to getting emphysema which made her bed-ridden with a 30-40% breathing capacity with three oxygen tanks weekly. My father continued to smoke while taking care of her. He claimed he could stop anytime he wanted, but he still smoked in the house instead of at least smoking outside. I didn't realize how much they smoked until we were cleaning some furniture after his death and saw the real color of the bedroom furniture! It was totally different from what we had always thought it was because of the nicotine smoke.

    I started writing poetry in the early 90s to combat the stupidity I kept hearing from the Liberals running our government. As I was going through some of my father's stuff I found that he had done some poems too and always in the name style of ABCB which meant the second and last lines rhymed and the poems I found were long ones over 12 quatrains in length. For example "A Poem About Italy Written at Foggia, Italy 1944" has at least 18 quatrains. For example:

> "We expected to have a barracks
> here our crew could live content,
> And then we hit this APO
> And our BOQ is a leaky tent.
>
> We floundered in a foot of mud
> And looked around the tent inside.
> The rats and mice glared back at us,
> And we were those who tried to hide."

I had known he could build nearly anything he wanted, draw well, do leather craft, and a myriad of other things, but he never really said anything about writing poetry. Another facet of a multi-faceted personality.

By the early 2000s I went to a poetry convention where I was honored with a glass stand and a blue globe. While I was there in Las Vegas I was enticed to self-publish my first book, *Birthed Thoughts About the Good, the Bad, and the Ugly*. Within it was a poem I had written about the horrors of sickle cell which I called, "**Being Well**"

"Globs, boogers, or even green slime,
The name of it doesn't matter this time
Only how it's colored and feels,
How tightly nose and lung it seals.
It stretches, retreats, and dangles,
Tantalizes and untangles
These sticky, green globs hang around,
Once dried, there's no more cough for thee to fear."

An Angel Departs I originally wrote after the mother of one of my students died suddenly of a bleeding ulcer leaving behind her husband and child who was fighting cancer. Over the years this poem has been adapted for each situation and loss. Of the some 500 poems I have penned, this one still stirs my emotions about that young mom and her family, all of whom I eventually was given the honor and responsibility of eulogizing.

> In her sleep a disembodied voice crooned,
> "Child, your labors here are finished."
> Avoiding the Heavenly voice she implored,
> "Not true for my son and husband need me."
> "Child, He who sent me has honored thy faithfulness
> In standing before Death, protecting your loved ones,
> All the works He began in you are finished,
> And He has bid me bring you to His throne."
> As her breathing ceased, she looked down below
>   And saw her husband shaking her trying to revive her.

Tears flowed from her heart in the anguish left
    behind,
"I can't leave, they need me so."
Child, you have poured your life into them both,
 Your faith and testimony have blessed the Father.
Your Lord Himself has prepared your mansion.
 In time both son and husband will join you there.

 Rising with the Heavenly messenger, she
asked, "Who will tell the story of my son?"
` "Whether it's him or a friend, matters not,
  But his story, as well as your own shall be known."
Taking a deep comfort from his words, this petite,
God fearing mother felt the burden leave,
 As she was led to the Son, who told her,
  "Well done, my good and faithful servant."

    Originally written to comfort the husband And the student I had at the time, every time I read or write these words, I remember the family and the circumstances that tried to tear that family apart. Then I thank God I was able to be a small part in ministering to them, for they surely blessed me.

Over the decades terminology has evolved as people needed a more concrete definition to fit the problems they encountered yet had a difficult time dealing with. As I sit here today, this type of personality when I was growing up has been neatly pigeon-holed conveniently as "obsessive-compulsive" disorders. This is just a fancy way of dealing with an age-old personality that was just thought of as being **strict** and nothing more. This do-as-I-say personality believes everything has its place including obedient children. Growing up I never doubted who the disciplinarian in our family was or whether or not that I'd be punished for breaking the rules of the house. My father was strict and believed in administering "the rod" to our butts for offenses real or imagined. Mother, who we loved, we knew we could talk our way out of most spankings, but if she had to pass the information on to dad about what we had done, he would get really pissed. First, that he had to do the discipline of stuff that had happened while he was not there, and secondly, that we had not obeyed mother. Then we went to our room, bent over the end of the bed and had his belt applied liberally to our butts! I know I screamed and cried, but can't remember if my brother gave Dad that satisfaction.

So Dad's strict discipline methods earned him a sort of grudging, fearful respect and we tended to use the same approach with our own children to a degree. This is not necessarily an endearing character trait, but then it was never intended to do anything but instill obedience, not mindlessness. I have even heard this instead: he was strong-willed, independent, bossy, often impatient especially if you couldn't grasp something the first time it was shown or explained to you. He was argumentative, goal-oriented, not easily discouraged even though he might be wrong for he was human. He was self-sufficient most of his life, quick-tempered, often vitriolic. He was domineering, rude, tactless, bored with the mundane, angered by hypocrites and incompetence. He couldn't say "I love you" because according to him and Webster, the word "love" was simply another form of "like." However, he did write me once and closed with "Love from your old man" He wrote this while he was fighting overseas during World War 2. He was also so unaccommodating that Mother made each of us promise to keep visiting him after she died. She knew he was not the easiest person in the world to get along with but she told us we did not know the man she had married, meaning that his experiences during the war had changed him. An example of what she meant was when they went to grab a bite to eat after he got back and a kid fired a cap pistol behind him in the cafeteria and laughed because of Dad's reaction. Then he told the kid's mom staring at her with those cold blue eyes that the next time a "GI with battle fatigue might just kill her brat."[**The Answered Call**", p. 68] We tried to keep our promise but we were in his home only by his acquiescence. Since there was no real conversation, after twenty minutes or so of one word answers, we had exhausted ourselves mentally and began mentally flagellating ourselves for perpetuating the torture we were permitting ourselves to be subjected to.

In many ways my father was a brilliant man, a very good artist and musician. He was blessed with being able to accomplish almost anything he wanted to do with his hands, and he thought everyone else should be able to do the same thing, especially his sons. His mechanical genius he displayed at a young age. His father raced boasts on Lake Michigan and my father was expected to take those high performance engines apart, fix any problems, and reassemble them correctly all without praise for a job well-done. He became an accomplished pianist, accordionist and organist to a lesser degree.

    As a child I my parents had enrolled me in an accordion school and was preparing for my first recital when Dad decided he had had enough of Chicago winters and moved the family to Fort Worth, Texas. Although they did try to get me a one-on-one instructor it just wasn't the same and was quickly dropped. Many years later, because his accordion was sitting in the hall closet gathering dust, I gathered my courage and asked him to teach me to play the damn thing. I should have known better because no matter how much I tried, I wasn't going to be good enough for him so eventually I gave up flagellating us both.

My sons and I get our artistic veins from him and the singing from his father who had sung professionally occasionally. Dad's art was in the form of cars and planes and of course nudes. He drew the cover for the yearbook **Wings** while training to fly along with the portrait of the officer winning his wings. He also did some cartoons in those periodicals.

I believe that part of his personality quirks can be ascribed to growing up in the dysfunctional family unit that he did. His mother was always an extremely nervous person and had separated or divorced grandpa several times. During these episodes, my uncle lived in Springfield with my Great Grand- mother Clara while my Dad had the more stable part of being in the same dysfunctional environment during his home life. So Lou was shunted around and joined the Army after graduating high school.

There is a streak of exhibitionist that runs through our genes. In my dad, he took to fencing and I suppose that he wished he had been born several hundred years earlier. He liked to show off for the girls walking down the halls of his high school on the way to the nurse's office with part of an epee sticking out of his neck and bleeding down the front of his shirt. My brother and I could play all sorts of street ball, but when he found out the softball team at school was not using the softball he thought, meaning soft and about six inches in radius, he pulled me from the sport fearing I'd get hurt. All my boys were allowed to compete of not depending on their choice.

      One of the pastimes that my family was involved in before the War was the Chicago Gun Club. My Grandfather had his own shooting range in the basement of his Berwyn home. It wasn't much, just a steel trap to catch the bullets from .38 pistol rounds. I saw many pictures of the gun rigs worn by my Dad and Uncle. They were range officers for the Club and with the holstered gun rigs, vests, chaps and hats they approximated what a suburban cowboy might have looked like. There was even a picture of my father posing in his garb and marked as having won a photo contest put on by Walgreens. Lou's girlfriend even got involved and dressed the part. I don't know why, but my uncle always wore a two gun rig. My Grandpa was elected the president of the club and presented a silver cigarette case inscribed with his life membership.

Just as my uncle escaped into the Army after high school, I also escaped. My Great Grandmother Clara was moving in with us. I didn't have the stomach for the black stuff under her fingernails or her poor hygiene and didn't want to be drafted into the Army as the Vietnam "war" was getting hotter so I enlisted in the Air Force expecting to get into electronics.

However I scored too well on one of the tests I was given, told I seemed to possibly have an aptitude for languages, and was being assigned to the Language school program. So after Basic at Lackland I was sent to Indiana University to learn Russian!

After nine months of intensive training, a stint at Goodfellow to learn the equipment I'd be using, I was sent overseas to the 6913th Security Sqn, which was stationed on an army base in Bremerhaven, Germany. After about thirteen months on the "Mox Nix" flight ,the bastardized motto of Able Flight which was "Das Mach Nicht" or "That doesn't matter." Then I was sent on "temporary duty assignment" to Tuslog 3-2 in Samsun, Turkey for the rest of my four year enlistment. "TDY" was hardly temporary as I was there over thirteen months doing what I had been trained to do: listening to Russian radio traffic.

Duane L. Schuman

While I was in Turkey several interesting things happened. First, one of our RB-66 Reconnaissance bombers went down in the Black Sea, which has sharks in it. We lost the three man crew and were only able to recover a piece of the tail section. Then one evening the Turkish military thought to invade our classified compound. When their vehicles were heard coming up our hill, everyone was issued weapons and live ammo and told what to do. For me that was groping outside in the dark with most of my flight, taking up combat positions in the grass, loading our weapons and chambering live rounds. We could hear the Turks talking to the Air Police at the entrance demanding to be let in and our boys denying them entry. This went on for about ten minutes. Then we heard the truck engines revving and departing. One crisis over and weapons unloaded and returned to the armory. While there we got to hear the Soyuz blast off as the space race had heated up. Ever since the Russians shot 'mir" into space the US was belatedly trying to catch up. I always thought it ironic that they chose to call this satellite 'mir' which meant both 'world' and 'peace.' Besides this space traffic we were on the alert for both bomber and fighter traffic and deployments. "Pust'" was a word we did not want to hear for it meant their fighters had fired a missile at another plane which at that time had to be American. It has only been since the Internet has become so widespread that I learned that my old unit in Germany, which fell under the aegis of the United States Security Service and the National Security Agency has its own web-site with info that would have been considered classified in the 60s and 70s!

    My Dad's first marriage to some broad named Agnes was a 30-day wonder that ended in divorce. It seems that her mother decided she needed to buy a new Frigidaire refrigerator which she wanted but consulted my Dad. He refused to buy "Cadillac" when "Ford" would do. Well when Dad came home from work, they argued and she brought up divorce. He told Agnes that if she was going to keep on doing what her mother wanted then she need to go home to her, which she did with a divorce soon to follow.

    Thinking back there appears to be some sort of dissociative personality disorder running through the male side of the Schuman line and most strongly felt by my father. Who was he? That was a question posed over and over again in his teen years because there is a question about the ending of the last name. Is it one or two "n's?" His social security card has Harry E. Schumann, school and military records have just the single "n."

He has signed his art as Ace Schuma**nn**, Harry Schuma**n**, Harry E. Schuma**n**, H.E. Schuma**nn**, H.E. Schuma**n**. His brother's social has one "n" but his high school diploma has two. These discrepancies seemed to appear around the time of George E. Schuman who was supposed to have originally have dropped the second "n."

I mentioned my father was goal oriented. Well he got the whole family involved in collecting coins in the late 50s. We'd cash in a $25 treasury bond to get a bunch of pennies and go through them to fill our penny books which escalated into nickel, dime, and quarters, and eventually half dollars. He got us involved with a coin bid board at the local coin store called Causey's. We each had our own bid numbers, but the only one I still remember is Dad's 63. Though the ownership of the shop would change hands, Dad still kept two safes on the premises. Because he got busy taking care of mother and getting old himself, he stopped checking on the safes. He had an inventory of everything that he put into them that did my brother and I no good when we discovered that the safes were empty! Apparently there had been an elaborate collusion between some of the "friends" who were helping the widow out running the store. The Haltom City police did catch two of the thieves with some of the stolen property still in their possession and we along with all the other safe renters who had lost property were invited down to identify our property, if we could. That was an impossibility. Since Dad had no coins that had been sent to a grading company and professionally graded and encapsulated it was impossible to say a certain coin was Dad's, a loss of almost $50,000 from our inheritance simply due to father's trusting the wrong people in the wrong situation, an abnormality for him. Like love, Dad did not trust people outside our family, and I am not sure he really trusted anyone, a circumstance that might have started during the war when Brock, his navigator flippantly mentioned he had forgotten his equipment that he needed for the trans-oceanic flight to Italy. This oversight actually caused my Dad to threaten Brock's life (see **The Answered Call, p.40**). I know what looking into those eyes of his when they seemed to turn ice-blue was like when I disappointed him.

As kids, my brother and I used to play mumbly-peg, throwing open pocket knives as close to the other's shoe as possible. This was an extension of the knife throwing Dad got us involved in. We had an old, partially rotting 2 x 12 some 12 foot long in the back yard. Since it wasn't much good for anything else, my Dad decided it would make an excellent backboard for knife-throwing. So he made a set of knives. Of their 12" length only 4 ½" was the haft or handle with the rest the blade. Only the tip was sharpened on both sides. The handle was three layers thick of the same steel he made the rest of the knives out of. They were nicely balanced for throws of 10, 15, and 20 feet. It wasn't long before my brother and I also gravitated to using them in our mumbly-peg. However, that stopped after I put a knife through the tip of my brother's shoe. We also got into other mischief with knives and blowguns. I don't know why, but we used to take steak knives and stab the edge of the pantry door in the kitchen when the parents were out. Occasionally we also did it in the kitchen cabinets above the sink. Those cabinets were made of fir and it's possible that damage was never discovered. I don't remember ever getting spanked for it anyway. A blowgun entered our lives but there was a problem. The blowgun didn't come with enough darts so Dad showed us how to make extras using coat hangers, cotton and clear fingernail polish to harden it. We would straighten the wire hangers and cut off lengths of either 5 or 6 inches. The wire cutters made instant points then take a cotton ball , swirl it into shape on the length of metal and apply the nail polish and let it harden. The result was another blowgun dart! Since we could have as many darts as we wanted to make, we needed something to shoot at, inanimate objects grew bland very quickly. Then we discovered toads! Those suckers couldn't be killed by simply shooting them with a few darts. They'd still try to hop away to get out of range, even after we had re-captured them long enough to reclaim our darts, they just hopped away, leaving us to other devilment.

Growing up like I did with the family unit I was in, I had an invisible "chip on my shoulder" syndrome just looking for a victim. In the second grade it was a kid named Forbes who was my nemesis. For some reason I no longer recall, he agreed to fight me on my own turf after school. The only reason I remember this at all is probably because it was my first fight, and I was winning. Suddenly, Forbes cries for time out to tie his shoe! And my dear sweet mother who was outside watching us, made me let him! The minute my attention was diverted by my mother, Forbes ran away! The second non-familial incident occurred as I walked to school. As I walked down Wheeler on my way to Oak Knoll Elementary I had to pass this house on the corner of Wheeler and Clarence. There was a brat who used to berate me and sometimes throw rocks at me. This time he said he was going to hit me. I told him if he did, I'd split his head open with it.

Right, you guessed it. The brat hit me in the back so I picked up the same rock, spun around and chunked it right back…and hit him in the head! By the time I got to school his big brother was there talking to the principal about me splitting his brother's head open.

She sent him on his way. And Natha Howell, the principal of the school that now bears her name asked me what had happened so I told her, omitting nothing. She admonished me, as one of her "Patrol Boys" to set a better example and that was that.

During this time I and my brother had our differences which he would generally end as the victor either then or at a later date when he ambushed me. I don't really know why I picked on him, because I knew he would lay for me until he was satisfied retribution had been accomplished. All of this was done without Pa's butting in.

My brother has a phenomenal memory, especially when it pertains to whatever our father has done to us. To him it was abuse. To me it was a spanking, not a beating. Now, it no longer matters as the "perpetrator" is dead and I am in my 70s.

Another aspect of my own vitriolic nature occurred in Germany during my first tour. I had another airman who just got his kicks heckling me while I was trying to listen to classified traffic. I had repeatedly warned him to leave me alone. On this day during a particularly difficult intercept he decided to screw around with me again. But this was the wrong time. I simply yanked my typewriter out of my kiosk and threw it backwards over my head at him. Anyone who was up was quiet! I got up, went and got my typewriter which was undamaged, replaced it back in my kiosk, put paper back in it picked up my earphones and got back to work. Nothing was ever said to me by anyone about the incident.

Thinking about my role in our family I realize now that I could never have lived up to my father's expectations for He was the model that I could not surpass in art, poetry, mechanics, playing any instrument, chess, card games, anything requiring dexterity or eidetic memory.

However I did manage to accomplish one feat that escaped my father: I graduated college with a B.A.! The most he had accomplished was some junior college- because he could not pass calculus! For some reason this math subject stumped him and he took it twice that I was told.

However that one incident was enough to let me know that I needed to be extremely cautious since I must have inherited my father's volatile temper, which could cause me no end of trouble in the future if I was not particularly careful. So far, I have only unleashed it in my stories.

Chalk Dust Memories
Part Three: Pet Peeves

One of the major gripes I have now and had as a teacher is standardized testing, especially District wide, mandated tests. Whether it was the pre-90s TEAMS [Texas Educational Assessment of Minimum Skills]; its successor TAAS 1991-2002 [Texas Assessment of Academic Skills]; the TAKS [Texas Assessment of Knowledge and Skills] from 2003 and the new STAAR [State of Te3xas Assessment of Academic Readiness] which is the current testing instrument. What parents have apparently not been aware of is that the scoring has been altered every succeeding year so that the same score that passed a student one year would fail the following years students is they did not improve a certain number of percentage points or they will fail because they fall below the curve. Traditionally a 50% score passes but the following year it will take a 55 to pass and the third year a 60. It's the old shell game with a new twist, except it is the students and the teachers who are the victims. Districts will find it more and more difficult to fill the 3, 4, and 5 grade slots with excellent teachers as their jobs are tied to this test. Have you ever seen some of the textbooks a high school subject is supposed to cover, much less master? It has become like a college class, without college credit with a maximum of 90 hours of instruction per subject per semester with actual instruction closer to 70 hours plus tests, etc.

There used to be a radical idea in education: learn what is taught! It doesn't matter how you learn it, just learn it. If you are a visual learner and can read the information and know it good for you! If you learn better by having the information presented to you auditorially and then you know it that is fine! If you learn better taking notes to bring in other modalities, great! Just make the attempt to pay attention and don't disrupt the learning of others!

`Another pet peeve is someone who abuses their authority for whatever reason. In particular, I had a boss who lorded it over me for some reason. She didn't like the fact that I had given a particular special education student 50-s, which she discovered going through my grade-book during one of her "teacher evaluation talks". She told me that 65s would convey the fact to him that he had failed just as easily as 50s. It didn't matter that his actual average was 17 because he did virtually nothing for me. She ordered me to change the grades in my grade book, which is an official District document. I made certain that is what she wanted before I did so right in front of her. Then I wrote on one the pages why the grades had been changed on the document itself! After meeting with all the other Homebound teachers and telling them I was going to our teacher organization to grieve what had happened since she had flagrantly usurped my authority over a student by ordering me to alter an official document. In Texas, teachers can't unionize and strike, but they can't forbid us the right to join with each other similar to a union. Once the process started, it wasn't long before she was moved from our Department and her problems continued to mount. Even months later she would complain to me that I was the one who stabbed her in the back to which I would simply remind her that her own mouth was her undoing as I walked on by.

In addition to these. another pet peeve I have is hypocrites. Say what you really think and be done with it, I may not agree, but I will respect you for being truthful. I realize that society forces us to wear masks in order to blend in with the norm, but if you are going to give me your opinion on something, be honest about what you tell me or say nothing at all.

Then there is the healthy person who takes up the parking space of a handicapped person because they are too damned lazy to walk a few steps! I wish to God that I had the ability to walk those spaces. Unfortunately most stores don't wasn't to do any- thing about these morons, although they could be ticketed for fraudulently misusing those decals, but generally, I can't find a cop available either. However, Texas is a right-to-carry state and it won't be long before you hear in the news, "Irate handicapped shopper shoots healthy bozo for taking his parking spot thinking the decal was permission to park in that space even though it wasn't issued for him personally. The shooter has been quoted as having asked the victim where his decal was and why he a healthy person needed to park there to which he was supposedly told oh it's on the kitchen table for my crippled aunt at which time the enraged handicapped person shot and killed him."

Then there are the church goers who are always quick to complain or offer their unsolicited opinions on everything, however when volunteers are needed to implement any changes, they seem to disappear into the woodwork. They are very self righteous, and their key word is self. They seem to avoid doing anything positive, such as being a member of a committee because that might cut into their "me" time. This personality is loud, boisterous, confrontational, often lonely, nursing a grudge or grief, and needs empathy and forgiveness.

Then there is the pet peeve about drive-through server which gets your order wrong. If you are alone in a long line of honkers, you can't generally open everything right there to make certain the cretin giving you the order gave you what you asked and paid for. You see the signs about speedy service from you pay window for the order you are asked to pull up and park and wait. I wouldn't be surprised in this day of violence to hear a person got the wrong order and in frustration rammed the car in front which had been parked waiting for a simple order of French Fries when he was rammed and thrust out into oncoming traffic where he didn't have to wait for service anymore!

  So, if your pet peeve falls into the category of the toilet seat up or down, toothpaste squeezed in the center or not; toothpaste, capped or not; dishes rinsed or not; beds made or not; car tank refilled after being borrowed or not; new book with pages dog-eared or not; or thousands of similar minor things that you call peeves, you are one of the lucky ones. Jump up and down and thank God that you do not have a child with severe special needs who will have to be looked after his entire life by--- you guessed it, you. In this life there are peeves and there are PEEVES. The latter are challenges that would try every saint to live through without being bitter. I have my talents, but those are not the kind God engendered to me. For those with that type of child be thankful for God saw something special in your soul when He created you, knowing in advance that He could place that special child with a special parent.

Duane L. Schuman

Chalk Dust Memories
Stand Outs: Old Teachers

In everyone's life there are people who stand out for some reason or another, and for me the teachers I had were no exception. When we first moved to Texas in 1951, I was put in Mrs. Bellamy's third grade class. She was a ball of cheer that all these years afterwards I can still visualize. She was a portly, robust teacher not much taller than I was. Her jowls shook when she laughed, which was often. She had learning games available for students who finished their assignments early so I made certain I was able to partake of them.

Fourth grade was different because the teacher was single. Miss Wilson seemed pretty because she used a lot of make up trying to disguise a horrible case of acne and I can still smell the cloying scent of it and see the silk scarf she perennially wore around her neck.

I don't remember my fifth or sixth grade teachers at all. When I went on to junior high school the only seventh grade teacher I remember was my English teacher, Mrs. Simons. She believed in vocabulary development and increasing one's reading speed and used a special edition of **The Readers Digest** geared for that. She was also my ninth grade teacher.

For eighth grade I remember Mrs. Boone, who was a direct descendant of Daniel Boone. Since I made A's in her English class, when she went to the high school, I followed and made sure she was my English teacher every year.

Those are my stand outs. Although I might recognize a name or two more from high school or college nothing stands out.

Chalk Dust Memories
Death Intrudes

In the summer of '62, I was still 16, but mother knew her father was dying and made the decision to try to see him one last time before then, if possible. So we loaded up the Ford station wagon and she had me with my new driver's license drive while she sat in the front passenger seat. My brother rode in the back.

In '62 there was no freeway north to Illinois, just highway which was two lane in both direction with a lot of one lane traffic thrown in for good measure making for a lot of passing and pulling back into your lane before oncoming traffic closed the lane. I remember I had to peg the car twice to get back into my lane in time. We made fairly good time even with the four hours it took to go through St. Louis, there not being any loop around back then.

Suffice to say we did get to see mother's dad for a few moments a piece before he passed. Grandma told us he was holding on just to see his grandsons one more time then he could relax. I actually heard his last breath leave his tortured lungs-seemed somewhere between a wheeze and a whistle. He had been laying on his back for so long half his eyes appeared to have been worn away. He died from emphysema which would years later kill my mother too. We went to the viewing, but weren't allowed to go to the burial because my aunt convinced my mother we were too young to be involved in death. What she meant was she didn't want her son to see it, so we waited across the street having ice cream sundaes while the funeral went on.

Chalk Dust Memories
Thinking Back

Whenever you think back, you never really know where your thoughts will take you. Sometimes it becomes easy to get bogged down in the negatives of the past; the I wish, the I hads; or the what ifs. Well, this is about the greater role of my mother.

She was a caring, intelligent and loving person. In addition to running the household on the meager money dad left while he was out of town selling business machines, she developed life-long correspondence with relatives and friends they had made over the years; sewed elaborate doll dresses for neighborhood girls; learned to make hats with one of her friends; played all sorts of card games; and became the care-giver to Dad's grandma first and then to his father. I know she was bitter somewhat about the latter because that prevented her from being able to take care of her own mother. She never blamed my father for continuing to fill the house with smoke after she became ill; for not having been able to live in a good house instead of the cinder block house we did live in, or for being riffed, instead she always tried to lift his spirits. When he started working with builders, she never complained that he left her alone. Instead she pointed out the he made her a sandwich, made sure she had a thermos of coffee, a phone nearby and could watch the tv. In the later years she'd write him about her thanks that he put up with her. Yes Mom, you were the shining light of our family

In every family there are similarities and differences and as I thought about it I recognized some of them:

Musically inclined	both Dad and Lou play piano and organ
	Dad play accordion
Sang	professionally Buck
Chain smokers	Dad, Lou, Buck
Wife's death	Dad-mom emphysema
	Lou- Albie heart
	Buck-Mabel hypertension
He died of	Dad cancer throat/stomach
	Lou heart
	Buck Parkinson's/heart
Children	Dad 2 sons
	Lou childless
	Buck 2 sons
Marriages	Dad div and marry Mom
	Lou just marry Albie
	Buck div remarry Mabel
Care-giver	Dad Mom-Clara and Buck
	Lou-Leigotts and Albie
	Buck no
Expect perfection	Dad, Buck
Dog lover	Dad, Buck small
	Lou collies
Presbyterian	Dad baptism, mil/y records
	Lou baptism mil/y records
	Buck went when lived here

Games	Dad-cards, chess, cribbage
	Lou-cards
	Buck cards??
Accident prone	Dad epee in throat., fell off
	ladder crush bones heel
	Lou fell off ladder at work
	Buck cut off part of thumb

Chalk Dust Memories
Me and Religion

Although my parents did not raise me in any specific denomination I always considered myself a Christian without really understanding what that entailed.

My earliest experiences with organize religion were with a non-denominational church where our Boy Scout troop met and stored our equipment. My Dad would drop my brother and me off on Sundays for Sunday School and pick us up when it was over. When our troop disbanded that church seized our equipment saying since they let us meet it belonged to them.

In basic training going to church was optional but I did go when a certain Episcopal priest was speaking. He seemed to have a direct line to God that I could understand at age 17. It wasn't until I got married in '68 that God started chasing me again. In our first apartment opposite Greenbriar Elementary two men came visiting and led us both to the Lord. Later we were both baptized at James Avenue Baptist Church. We tried it but it was geared for seminary students so we moved on in search of a church that met our needs.

Over the years there have been some Assembly of God churches, several Baptist churches, the Calvary Cathedral, The Fellowship of Love Outreach (FOLO), a gay church, a spiritual church plus some others until WPC. Little did we realized the background there was of Presbyterianism in my family line.

Always looking trying to listen to the Holy Spirit as He leads. And everywhere we went I gathered a skill or protection I would use dealing with my students from counseling them and their parents about God and His purpose to avoiding the snares the devil sets such as the wiccan philosophy. Psychic readings scotographs and other such drivel are tools used to mislead those seeking answers not found in this world.

Duane L. Schuman

Chalk Dust Memories
Hinterland Recall

Here I sit in the hinterland of my years having passed my seventy-first birthday. I have just realized that my days are truly numbered and my mortality looks back at me from the mirror.

No longer can I think Death is years away since Clara, my great, grandmother lived to 96 and her mother Lydia Skeen to her nineties,. She would have lived longer if she hadn't broken her scrawny neck going down some rickety cellar stairs. Yeah, the patrilineal side of my family line have been long-lived with the exception of my Great Grandfather Louis who died of pneumonia as he crossed the Atlantic in the bowels of a troop ship during World War I. My dad, his brother, and their father all lived into their eighties so I have always thought of Death claiming me as something way off in the future. Well, guess what! The years have passed and Death now stands in the corner waiting for God to signal that he is done with me.

The tasks that He had planned for me, have been carried out. Three sons have been raised and they know our stance where our faith in God lies. We have raised them to know Him, know they accepted Him as Lord and no matter what society or culture dictates, I have faith they will join us in the after-life. The ministry planned with children who would die I carried out the last twenty-eight years of my teaching career, impacting many families as they impacted me.

I was blessed to know the one family who impacted my life more than all the others. Now able to look back, I know the eternal hand of the Lord was involved or I would not have had this student for so long, it just wasn't policy to keep a student for such a long time because of the attachments formed. I only know God kept me involved with this family for six years since He knew they would need someone to buoy up their faith, listen to their hopes, dreams, and worries. Yes, Cathy and Randy needed to hear positive words about Eric and not the negative prognoses the oncologists offered. Sop soon after meeting them they trusted me enough to ask me to get an elder to anoint their son with oil had a profound effect upon my own outlook then and even now as I bring the same rite to Westminster showing the pastor that a "Healing Service" is a valid rite even today in today's Presbyterian church. Over the years I managed to get Eric involved in his writing once more and they became involved in my own. His mother was the first to edit my first book, **Battlefields of the Mind** some fifteen years or so ago. As the years passed the bond between the members of that family and me strengthened to the point that upon Cathy's untimely death from a bleeding ulcer I was asked to give an eulogy for her and that is how the poem "An Angel Departs" came into being. Used first for her, it has been used several times over the years at the passing of other students and individuals. So, Cathy rest easy for I have told the story of your son and your whole family and people get blessed over and over after reading some of the things I kept that Eric wrote about how he dealt with his cancer. One truly brave son, and an extraordinary family I was blessed to have had a small part in their lives.

    I realize that my poetry is not for everybody. Heck, my wife doesn't like most of it or understand any with secondary messages. Being out of the work force has taken away the one subject which seemed to always give me something that stirred my emotions to write about. However, I have not been idle. I have been finishing several stories I had started in the 90s as well as some novels. I have some available through Amazon.

    I have come to understand that my writing is mainly a facet of my need for self-expression. It no longer matters whether the composition is fiction, science fiction, western, paranormal, memoirs or some other genre. Since I am really writing for myself, what the hell does it matter? No one else really cares. No one cares enough to read what I write to know me better. Though I don't pound the keys of an 88, my thoughts to encapsulate like a pianist would, my keyboard output stirs my emotions as they seek an outlet whether it be science fiction trilogy, western mad-dog killer or western come to God or even a version of these memoirs. So currently under construction are the following: "**The Quick Hand of Death**" a western I started in the 90s is basically finished. It has a few graphic sex and violence scenes not for the feint-hearted**;**" **Rolling Thunder**", another western with a religious bent which is now finished and available from Amazon**;** "**Double Trouble**" the 2nd in the Battlefields series is completed just working the kinks out of the proof; "**Chalk Dust Memories**" which is memoir-like, sort of; "**Lifeforce**" is science fiction and basically complete; "**The Prophet**" is another sci-fi which is nearly complete. Then there is "**The Pestilence**" which is the working title of the third book in the Battlefields series.. It has been birthed and then shelved for the time being. Then there are other writings I am not sure what I will do with them. "**The Victimized**" is a murder/sci-fi which is currently just a short story. Then there is "**The Unknown Prophet**" which is hard to describe its genre. It could be a religious think piece or the start of something else. "**The Presence**" is basically sci-fi.

 I have noticed that I have drawn upon my memories in different writings. Growing up I was a member of a psychic church where I got several ideas about the occult, ouija boards, scotographs, witchcraft, Anton Levy's Satanic Bible, séances, seers, and a plethora of similar shit. Some of the things that happened at school did indeed occur: Russian roulette on the parking lot, rapes in school, fights galore, teachers intervening in fights, students bringing all sorts of weapons to school and using them, use of profanity gained use from 80s thru 2009 when I had to retire. I have come into contact with incense burning Wiccans, witches but no warlocks, pyromaniacs, murderers, supremacists, racists, bigots, bullies, and just a bunch of mean-spirited individuals, their families, and of course their victims. From them, their conversations, and being in their home environments various truths came into light from which I have garnered bits and pieces as I needed them into various story lines, giving them an air of authenticity.

    Kids who are left alone too much have too much time they can put their negative thoughts into reality. It might be something small in the area of self-mutilation. This is an area often over-looked by parents if they do not see visible signs; but why draw unwanted attention to oneself it you can't draw positive feedback you desire? Here the quiet kid can slowly experiment upon his own body without anyone knowing what he is doing if he is careful. Even sewing straight pins seems so innocuous can be inserted slowly to the head up to a depth of a inch and a quarter and apparently cause little in the way of discomfort or evidence of blood loss.. As a kid I know we used to put straight pins on our arms in the crease on the inside of the elbow and slowly "make a muscle" impaling the pins into our arms!

Back in the 70s and 80s kids were killing themselves by senseless asphyxiation. Rope and twine or heavy cord have always been a tool of those with too little parental discipline and affection. Back then a lot of youths died trying to approximate the rush they felt came with sexual release, greater than just masturbating. Too many guessed wrong and put themselves in inescapable positions such as hanging from a bathroom door. They strangled them- selves to death trying to reach a sexual high.

So the role many parents abrogated was soon filled by the gangs. Here the kids felt a bonding, a kinship with someone who understood what they felt. Unfortunately these gangs usually ended up on the wrong side of the law or killed by someone since drugs or guns usually became involved. .

While I taught on one side of town, the police might be storming a house on the other side by a school my wife was teaching at as they looked to bust a drug dealer. Some of the students admitted in their writings that they were involved with drugs, usually on the side of being users and one admitted to being in a gang as he was the object of a drive-by shooting..

When I grew up in the 50s, drugs and gangs were mostly unheard of, certainly not as prevalent as they are in the neighborhoods of today. Now, they seem to be glorified in the media with all sorts of tv shows depicting police or SWAT raids upon suspected dope drops. The teens of today fixate on what is put before them so putting all this on tv doesn't alleviate the problem it exacerbates it in the adolescent mind. And now some states are legalizing medical marijuana. How long will it take susceptible teenagers to find ways to obtain it?

Not long ago I observed an advertisement online for a shirt for veterans with a statement about the oath we took.

Thinking it over I realized that the truth of the statement "I took an oath to defend the Constitution against all enemies foreign and domestic. Be advised that no one has ever relie4ved me of my duty under this oath."

For my children who can't understand my aversion for the Secretary of State who used her own server for e-mails instead of the encrypted government one thus abrogating her oath. It has nothing to do with her political persuasion. It has everything to do with her trashing an oath millions of us have taken and many shed their blood over. She had no reason to do what she did except she thought she was above her oath and beyond any accountability. Hopefully the bitch did no irreparable damage and no lives were lost by her actions but only time will tell.

Duane L. Schuman

Printed in Dunstable, United Kingdom